WORKBOOK: HACKING KICKSTARTER, INDIEGOGO HOW TO RAISE BIG BUCKS IN 30 DAYS

SECRETS TO RUNNING A SUCCESSFUL CROWD
FUNDING CAMPAIGN ON A BUDGET

PATRICE WILLIAMS MARKS

BOOK TRAILER

Watch the book trailer by CLICKING IMAGE.

REVIEWS

"*Hacking Kickstarter is the Bible for all those who want to kick start their crowd-funding project. The author, Patrice Williams Marks, has done a lot of research. She has identified readily available and cheap but powerful media technology tools to make your project successful.*"

"*If you've had a failed campaign take a look at Patrice*

Williams Marks' book for examples on how to turn things around. This book is great for those who need ideas as it has examples and tips on how to get back on your feet."

"I give this two thumbs up and a 5/5 review score."

Night Owl Reviews - Top Pick

"I haven't finished the book yet, and already I believe there is more content than expected - which is a pleasant surprise. I'm an attorney teaching crowdfunding, and some of this content [will] definitely be added to our marketing section and I will recommend the purchase of the book."

Divina Westerfield, Esq.

"HACKING KICKSTARTER, INDIEGOGO: HOW TO RAISE BIG BUCKS IN 30 DAYS! You will be given a full arsenal of practical ideas on organizing media lists, posting videos that can target heavy traffic, creating personal links, and manipulating crowd funding to its fullest potential."

Rachel Aderholdt

"Patrice, you provided a detailed "how to" book that is truly unrivaled."

DreamScriber "Joshua Cintron"

"If you have a project you want funded, this is a must read."

Love 4 Books Blog

"This is a five star book for sure."
Athena L Nagel, The Stuff of Success Blog

PROLOGUE

This is the workbook version of the bestselling Hacking Kickstarter, Indiegogo crowdfunding book. You will complete fill-in forms and assignments which will help you immensely in developing and launching your successful crowdfunding campaign.

NOTE: For the sake of brevity, I will mostly refer to crowdfunding projects as Kickstarter Projects; although the information contained in this book will work with **ANY** crowdfunding site such as Indiegogo, GoFundMe, etc.

Also, this book is most useful for those who have yet to launch their crowdfunding project. However, if you have already, it is not too late to give yourself an added boost.

You also do not have to implement all of these suggestions to have fantastic results. Simply pick and choose the ones that work for you. **However, make sure you implement everything listed under: WHAT EVERY CROWDFUNDING PROJECT SHOULD HAVE.**

Dedicated to my sisters Phyllis, Wendy & Erica.

CASE STUDY

AMANDA PALMER

Heard of Amanda Palmer? You should have, but if not, let me fill you in. Amanda was an unknown musician/artist who had been quietly working in obscurity creating music for her niche fan base of punk/burlesque lovers. She decided she wanted to release a full-fledged studio album and tour the country, but she was an indie artist without the big bucks or record label behind her to do so. However, this didn't stop her. She decided to raise a few dollars though Kickstarter.

Her goal was $100,000 for a new record, art book and tour. She put a campaign together that included a highly-imaginative video showing a series of cue cards. She set the stage by using her own music as the background. The video not only showed her personality, but led us into her world. Even if you never heard of her before, you were intrigued.

So did she reach her goal? Amanda raised a whopping $1,192,793. It still stands as the largest crowd-funded music project to date.

So you must be thinking that *she must have had a marketing/pr background, had a lot of rich friends.* Not even close. What was her day job for many years? She stood on top of a box crate wearing a wedding dress, skin painted white- a living statue. She called herself the "8 foot Bride." When someone put money in her can, she would give them a flower, along with intense eye contact.

Yes, she was one of THOSE people that you either love, or go out of your way to avoid.

This is not the type of background that lends itself to raising one million dollars in 30 days. Or is it?

When she'd give someone a flower, she would also

exchange extended stares, as if to say, "*I see you, thank you.*" Sometimes we would receive, "*I am never seen, thank you.*"

Those direct, compressed connections between strangers is where she created her own unique "ART OF ASKING."

How else did she accomplish the "art?" After concerts, she and her bandmates would stay to connect with the audience. Before the show, she invited other artists, musicians, to set up outside of the gigs. They'd pass the hat, then join her on stage. That's how she created her community.

When Twitter came along, she would use that to reach out to fans by asking for random things like a piano to practice on in Auckland, NZ, or a meal and a place to crash in Seattle. Her "tribe" came though for her, as she had for them on many occasions, with spontaneous concerts, or free music giveaways.

She explains it as "an exchange between her and her fans," and "trusting each other."

It's all about the connections forged prior to your

project launch. If you have that base, they will carry you across the threshold and you will surpass your original goal.

So how do you make this happen? Read on.

What other successful crowdfunding campaigns have you heard about?

_____

_____

_____

_____

How did you hear about them?

_____

_____

_____

INTRODUCTION - STATS

So you have this great idea for a book, video game, water hovercraft, app, newfangled watch, dance project, but you don't have the money to produce it.

You've heard about this new thing called "crowd-funding" and believe this will be your ticket. Simply post a project to any number of sites and the money will begin to roll in, right? Wrong.

Unfortunately, according to a Kickstarter representative, "Only 44% of projects get funded."

So you think 44% is pretty good odds. Well, not when you look into the fine print. It depends on the category. 44% funded is based on the successes of dance projects. How many of us have one of those in need of funding?

Technology projects only fund 33%. Publishing, around 35 and Fashion funds the lowest, around 25%.

· · ·

The numbers come close to the same percentage on other sites as well.

See chart below by <u>Gigaom.</u>

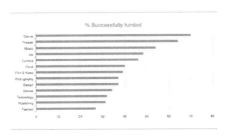

In the last six months of this report, there were 76,909 Kickstarter projects launched.

So how easy do you think it is to stand out in a crowd of thousands? Not easy at all.

But there is hope!

Right off the bat, how do you think your project can stand out in a crowd?

_____

_____

_____

_____

_____

_____

Bookmark your answer and refer back to it once you complete the workbook. Does the above response still hold true? Why or why not?

___ YES

___ NO

Why/why not?

_____

_____

_____

_____

_____

_____

I know there is hope because I have studied successful Kickstarter projects and found similarities. I've spent over 220 hours of research compiling this information in order to make my own Kickstarter Project a winner.

So how did I do?

I posted my project in the "under-funded" category of publishing. I wrote a short noir/futuristic story called, *The Unfinished*, which was having success online as an ebook. However, readers wanted the full novel. I decided to get a little support from strangers and created a Kickstarter project. I launched it without fanfare, but pulled the project shortly after as my next novel was consuming my time.

But, I decided to help others launch successful projects by sharing what I have learned.

This book is NOT a guide on how to put your Kickstarter project together, nor is it a basic overview of crowdfunding. (Find extensive FAQ, videos on their sites, as well as Kickstarter School resource.

I'll briefly mention what your project should have, but the aim of this book is to help you draw fans to your project and get them to open up their wallets.

I want your project to be in the 44% winner's circle!

WHAT EVERY CROWDFUNDING PROJECT SHOULD HAVE

• **A Video.** If you can afford to put a professional one together, do it. If not, sit in front of your computer and talk to us about what your project is about, what it means to you, how the money will be used. Also, thank the viewers/funders and mention the perks they'll get for their support. Humor ALWAYS helps.

How will you put your video together? What 3 main points will you make?

_____

_____

_____

- 1._____
- 2._____
- 3._____

• **A Website.** If you know how to set one up, do it. Be sure to get a personal URL, rather use a generic one from a free hosting site. Ex: www.yourhostname.com/yourprojectname. Perception is everything. Spend the $12 and buy a proper URL from Google Domains, (or anyone else). You don't want to come off as someone who doesn't know what he or she is doing. The website doesn't have to be extensive. It can even be a one-pager. Just include information on you, the project, updates and a way to sign up for the newsletter. *Wordpress* has quite a few free templates that are clean, simple and ready to roll. Bluehost; *(affiliate link), a company that I have been using since 1998,* is also a well-known and outstanding company for hosting websites and Wordpress sites with free 24/7 support in the USA.

Checklist:

- ___ Purchased website name
- ___ Created website
- ___ Added email list signup
- ___ Included ways to reach you

Want an example of a winning website? The Ripple (http://www.thefirstripple.com/); the world's first detachable bowl and plate. Why is it so great? The video that explains the product is front and center; images are crisp and very visual; they have tabs across the front of the website where you can read their story, buy, read press mentions, or contact them. They also had the Kickstarter logo in the center of their home page with a link to their project.

Also check out the crowdfunded game: *The 7th Continent.*   (https://www.kickstarter.com/projects/1926712971/the-7th-continent-what-goes-up-must-come-down) They raised over seven MILLION. The website promotes their backers on the home page (*as of the writing of this book*).

What did BOTH successful campaigns do on their home pages?

_____

_____

_____

_____

_____

• **Perks/Rewards.** Make them good. Period. Don't offer to give them a thank you on the Kickstarter website, or a postcard. People want something that is of value. They love sneak peeks, tangible goods. Give something away that is UNIQUE to your project. So what types of items should you offer as rewards? Do your research. Look up successfully funded projects (http://www.kickstarter.com/discover/categories/fiction/successful? ref=more%2523p1) *in your category* and see what they offered. **EXAMPLE:** You are offering a digital book download as a perk? Why not make it special by offering a *"digitally signed"* copy of the book? How do you do that? Simple. There is a **FREE** service called "AuthorGraph.com" where you upload your book and start sending out signed copies. The service allows for you to physically sign your signature using your finger or mouse. How cool is that? I also read a very helpful article written by Jason Boog on the MediaBistro/Galley-Cat website. (Reprinted with Permission.)

At the Digital Hollywood conference in Los Angeles, a group of successful Indiegogo and Kickstarter campaign founders shared advice at the "Crowdfunding Case Studies" panel discussion.

Sarah Weichel helped with the Indiegogo campaign for Hello, Harto (http://www.indiegogo.com/projects/hello-harto), raising nearly $223,000 to take a show on the road. She revealed that most fans wanted to spend between $20 and $50 for the campaign.

. . .

Weichel's campaign offered a number of perks, including buttons, t-shirts, doodles and other tangible rewards for backers. Weichel explained that the best perks should be customized and tangible: "[Fans] want something you have touched or made custom for them in some way."

In addition, pitcher and filmmaker Dave Blackburn shared this secret from his The King and Me (http://www.indiegogo.com/projects/the-king-and-me) campaign. He urged project founders to make a list of 50 people who will donate on the first day of your campaign. He ended up making a list of 300 people to contact. "That momentum will be huge for your project," he concluded.

Finally, Avital Levy used Jewcer.com to raise more than $8,000 for her Hummus Wars (http://jewcer.com/project/hummus-wars) project. She hosted the 1st Annual Hummus Cookoff to raise support for the project and urged creators to host a live event to raise awareness and engage supporters.

. . .

List at least 5 of your "unique" perks:

- I. _____
- 2. _____
- 3. _____
- 4. _____
- 5. _____

• **Pictures, Pictures, Pictures.** If you have pictures of your prototype, show it. Cover of your book, post it. A picture says a thousand words.

• **Testimonials.** Have supporters already? Have them write a quote and give you permission to use their full name. No quotes followed by "John from NY," as that comes across as phony. And yes, use your family and friends if you have to. What makes up a good quote? Short, sweet, detail-oriented. Example: *"Very cool ebook! I used it to help me raise $9,235 for my band's first album!"* **Michael Evans, Cool Band Name, Vancouver, WA.**

. . .

List at least 3 people or companies that will give you a testimonial:

- 1. _____
- 2. _____
- 3. _____

- **Multiple Ways to Contact You.** Make sure they can contact you outside of Kickstarter. Post an email address, free Google Voice (https://www.-google.com/voice) number that forwards to your cell (or any number). Make it easy for your potential funders to get a hold of you and see you as a real person. (Note: Chrome browser has a FREE plugin called Blur (https://goo.gl/3CWabr) which allows you to create masked email addresses and phone numbers to protect you from spam, as well as providing privacy protection).

List your contact information that is/will be on your website and crowdfunding page. (Phone numbers, emails, fax (yes, people still fax), social media accounts, etc.

_____

_____

_____

_____

_____

_____

_____

- **Post Your Bio and Picture.** We need to know who you are. We need a headshot.
Headshot Do's and Don't:

  - *Do wear appropriate (clean) clothing*
  - *Do wear solid colors*
  - *Do loosen up before the shoot*
  - *Do smile, be natural*
  - *Do have a professional background without distractions*
  - *Do take multiple shots from multiple locations*

  - *Don't force a smile*
  - *Don't use a photo with other people in it (unless they are part of the campaign)*
  - *Don't wear clothing with logos or distracting prints*
  - *Don't use outdated headshots*

- *Don't use a headshot which looks like a High School yearbook photo*
- *Don't wear too many accessories*

• **Tiers, Baby.** It's all about the tiers. Make sure you have at least 5 choices. Don't have the minimum rewards amount start at $100, or $50. People are more likely to feel comfortable donating at the $5 level.

List your tier level amounts:
Tier 1 Amount: $_____
Tier 2 Amount: $_____
Tier 3 Amount: $_____
Tier 4 Amount: $_____
Tier 5 Amount: $_____

• **Count the Costs.** If you plan on shipping items, be sure you know exactly how much that will cost and add to your funding dollar amount. Also take into account that around 10% of the money you raised will go towards Kickstarter and payment processor fees. So always ask for more than you need to cover the fees. (Read a horror story about one person who lost their home because of not es-

timating the actual costs)! http://www.patricewil-
liamsmarks.com/kickstarter-horror-story/

Let's figure out how much you should ask for:

- Amount you want to raise: $____
- Product design: $ - ____
- Photography of product: $ - ____
- Platform fees: $ - ____ (Factor in 10%)
- Product cost per unit: $ - ____
- Product fulfillment/shipping per unit: $ - ____ (be sure to calculate international shipping as well)
- Advertising: $ - ____
- Website, Social Media: $ - ____
- Misc expense: $ - ____

_____

Total Expenses: $ _____
Minus Goal Amount: $ _____
Equals: $ _____

Are your numbers adding up? Are you in the positive or negative? If in the positive, are you at your
goal? If not, rethink your expenses and goal. If you

are in the negative, you have to cut expenses and/or raise your goal amount.

• **Don't Ask For Too Much/Little.** Research similar projects and see what the going rate is. Asking for too much will turn people off. Too little, and you may find your project funded, but you're still in need of additional funds to fulfill the rewards. Don't put yourself in that position. You don't want to be that guy/girl who never fulfills their obligations. It will create bad will *and maybe lawsuits* that will be near impossible to come back from.

• **Find a Writer/Editor if You Aren't One.** No one wants to read a project description with a bunch of typos and misspellings. USE SPELL CHECK, but don't depend on it as your only editing tool.

• **Choose the right number of days the project will run for.** 30 day projects have the most success. Sure, your project can run longer or shorter, but why stack the cards against you?

· · ·

How long will your project run? Why?

_____

_____

_____

• **Close the deal.** Ask for their support; ask them to fund your project. Even President Obama ended every debate with, "I'm asking for your vote" when running for office.

• **Always keep your funders updated** throughout the project as they are now your partners and invested in your success. Active projects with frequent updates get more attention.

Okay, the list above is by no means complete, but I believe it will serve as a firm foundation to get you started.

If any of the above elements are missing from your project, all the advertising in the world won't help. What's the saying, "**slapping lipstick on a pig**"?

• • •

You get the idea.

So let's assume you've gotten your act together, you have a kick-butt project that is pending approval, or you're about to launch.

Fantastic.

3

DON'T LAUNCH UNTIL YOU HAVE ALL YOUR DUCKS IN A ROW... SERIOUSLY

I know you're excited to launch, but hold your horses. Premature launching can be disastrous if you aren't prepared. Thus, you don't want to be one of those 60% unfunded projects, do you? None of us want that. You bought this book for a reason and I intend to fully prepare you for battle.

And that's exactly what this is, a battle. A battle for success.

What do you think I mean by having all your ducks in a row? Respond below (*do not cheat and flip to the next chapter for the answer!*)

_____

_____

_____

_____

_____

4

GATHER YOUR TRIBE

This may be the single most dreaded tip I can give as it's not easy, it's time consuming and takes sweat equity.

. . .

What do I mean by gathering your tribe?

Just that. You need a LARGE GROUP of people who are waiting with bated breath for your launch. They've been prepped, informed several times and will carry you to the top on their collective shoulders.

How do you do this? You need a mailing list. You also need support from Twitter and Facebook.

Start with creating a mailing list **at least six months before your launch.**

I told you, you weren't going to like it.

The service **Prefundia.com** lets you post your project before it goes live; allowing it to gain momentum before the launch. People interested in your project register their email. Once your project goes live, Prefundia emails all the interested parties on your behalf. This service is currently free.

But don't just depend on this service to do your pre-marking. Prefundia is no guarantee that you will get email signups. You *must* make other outreach efforts.

MailChimp.com has a free service which is great for this. Start a mailing list by adding your friends and family. Ask them to forward newsletter invites to their friends, and so on. Visit forums, groups online, that would be interested in your project. Contribute to the conversation, then casually mention your mailing list and your project, with a link. NOTE: Be sure to use a signature line when registering for forums (include your mailing list link, website, etc.)

Mailerlite.com https://www.mailerlite.com/invite/891e0feb9e785 also has a free version and works like more expensive platforms for tagging subscribers, adding automation, the ability to send an email out at the exact same time, no matter what time zone you are in, etc. (*I use the paid version of this service. If you use the link above, you'll receive a $20 credit.*)

. . .

So you've created your website with a newsletter opt-in form on every page? Great. Now consider looking for a **pop-up service** to add to your Wordpress or regular website. To see one in action, visit my website: www.PatriceWilliamsMarks.com and click on the **RED BUTTON** on the home screen.

You've seen these before. You visit a site, then the page goes dark and a screen pops up asking you to join their newsletter list, or get a free download, etc. You join, or click out of it and finish viewing the page.

I used to think these were annoying to encounter, until I discovered that people who have them increase their newsletter subscriptions by 500%! Yes, 500%! Worth the effort? I think so.

So which ones should you use? The most popular one is Popup-Domination, but there are others that are less expensive. **Do a google search to find one that you and your wallet can agree on.**

. . .

Which pop-up programs are you considering?

_____

_____

_____

_____

Start a Twitter account just for your project. Find like-minded folks on twitter and follow them. They'll more than likely follow you back. Use your current social media accounts as well to gather your tribe. Tell them about your project and mailing list and, most importantly, ask them to RETWEET. Most strangers will retweet if you simply ask. Watch your tribe grow before your very eyes. Be sure to thank the re-tweeters and keep a running list of them. You'll also want to keep them updated on your project's progress.

Your new twitter account should be the name of your product or what it does. Write down a few ideas:

_____

_____

_____

_____

· · ·

Facebook.com: Add a new BUSINESS page for your project and be sure to create a custom name for the link to match your project. Ex: Facebook.com/YourProjectName. Find like-minded folks on Facebook and LIKE their pages, issue friend requests, etc.

Speaking of Facebook...

Consider placing a FACEBOOK AD advertising your new Facebook page, Kickstarter project, or both. Be sure to make the ad catchy and to the point. Use a photo with a large image so that the image can be seen easily.

Facebook ads are easy to get started and you can narrow down the reach to your target audience.

HINT: You can have the ad send people directly to your Kickstarter page.

Search online for $50 Facebook coupons to get you started for free. Sometimes you're able to find them offered on Fiverr.com for $5. (*Note: Be sure the seller has been on the site for several months and has a track record. Do not buy from someone who been there a month or less, as they may be scammers.)* Also, webhost providers like Bluehost offer discounts like this as well with hosting accounts.

Ignore the ads for people who say they will give you thousands of Twitter/Facebook/Youtube followers for $5. It's a scam. They use bots to falsely inflate the numbers, which quickly drop off after a week or two. **You want REAL PEOPLE following you, supporting you. (Twitter may also ban your account for illegal activity).**

There are so many other ways to grow your tribe, but they cost big bucks. If you can afford to print postcards and distribute, go for it! But I'll be focusing on free and low-cost ways to attract money to your project.

Don't forget about Pinterest.com. Pin relevant articles and photos associated with your project. Post, follow regularly and you will find an audience.

. . .

So when do you know if you have enough of a tribe to launch?

Let's just say that 100 people on an email list, 12 Facebook friends and a minuscule twitter list isn't enough. 500 is dandy, but 1000+ is optimum.

And don't just email them once. Keep them up to date, wanting more. Give new tidbits every 1-2 weeks leading up to the launch, then email them the day before launch, 3 days into the campaign, one week into the campaign, 2 weeks and with one week and 48 hours left. Always provide updated information and a call to action. Short and sweet and frequent.

List your email schedule and main message in 1-3 words:

    1. Date: _____ Message:_____

    2. Date: _____ Message:_____

    3. Date: _____ Message:_____

    4. Date: _____ Message:_____

    5. Date: _____ Message:_____

6. Date: _____ Message:_____
7. Date: _____ Message:_____
8. Date: _____ Message:_____
9. Date: _____ Message:_____

Once you have your tribe in place, give them the **hidden URL** to your Kickstarter *preview link*. Only those you share the link with will have access to it. Your supporters will be able to see your project BEFORE it officially launches. Ask for advice, suggestions from your tribe. They'll appreciate the "sneak peek" and you'll get valuable advice on tweaking your project before it's out there for the masses to consume.

NOTE: Once you launch your project, the preview link automatically forwards to the permanent project link location.

Speaking of links...

Create a *cleaner direct link* to your project for postings in your newsletter, online, media outreach, etc. Kickstarter links can be too long and cumbersome. URL shortening links are ugly (although I use them in this book!), give no hint of the project name.

Learn how in the next chapter.

5

HOW TO CREATE A PERSONAL LINK

For those of you who already have websites set up for your project, simply create a forwarding link to your Kickstarter project.

Example: YourProjectname.com/fund (People clicking on the link should be taken to your Kickstarter project). To do this using Bluehost.com:

1. Log into your account

2. Look Under "Domains" Heading closer to bottom of page

3. Select REDIRECTS

4. Select the domain name you want, (ie the Kickstarter website you created) from the drop down menu

5. After the "/" type in the name of the page you want to add, (I used "/fund" in the example)

6. You will see a box that says "Redirects to:"

7. You type in, or paste the full URL of your Kickstarter project

8. Click ADD button

9. You're done - YourProjectname.com/fund will now automatically re-direct to your Kickstarter page

If you don't have a website and don't plan on taking my advice to create one ... simply buy a do-

main name for $12 from Google Domains and
have the main URL forward to your Kickstarter
page.

6

POST YOUR VIDEO(S)
EVERYWHERE

Don't just post your Kickstarter video on their site.
Post it to as many sites as you can. Be sure to give a

detailed description of your project and launch date with each posting. List all your links, including your email list.

Important places to post your videos:

• Youtube.com

• Vimeo.com

• Behance.net An *under-utilized resource*

• Your Facebook Page

• Your Twitter Feeds

• Your Linkedin Profile Page or Business Page

• Pinterest Post

. . .

• Forums

• SnapChat (do a live stream)

• Friends Facebook Pages (*share to their page, but get permission first*)

Brainstorm other unique places you can post your videos:

_____

_____

_____

_____

_____

_____

NOTE: There is an interesting article from **Buzz-Feed** creator, Jonah Peretti, on 13 Ways To Make Something Go Viral. (http://www.facebookstories.-com/stories/1942/essay-13-ways-to-make-something-go-viral)

They are:

* Have a Heart

* Content is About Identity

* Make Content You Would Share Yourself

* Do not Focus on Tricks

* Be Yourself

* Try Lots of Ideas

* Capture the Moment

* Cute Animals Deserve Respect

. . .

* Humor is Inherently Social

* Do not Ignore Mobile

* Nostalgia is Inherently Social

* Human Rights Are Inherently Social

* Do not Post Things People Are Embarrassed to Share

In other words, create content that is sharable. Remember this every time you promote your project through Twitter, Facebook, blogs, videos, etc.

7

CREATE A MEDIA LIST

You could go about this the easy way by finding a paid service online that either writes and distributes, or just distributes, your press releases.

. . .

There are some free press release services, however, you cannot target your audience. However, free is a very good price!

There are paid services, of course, and they can get a little pricey. If you do a SEARCH on TWITTER for *CROWDFUNDING, CROWD-FUNDING, KICKSTARTER or INDIEGOGO* you will come across quite a few businesses who claim to promote your Kickstarter, Indiegogo project. Prices range from flat fees of $50 to $100 a week. I've never used any of these services, so I can't recommend any one over the other. However, research them, look at their Facebook page, Twitter account. If they are inactive, seem spammy, post meaningless tweets that would never generate traffic, (I've seen one tweet from such a company that simply said: "Good Project" with a link to the campaign) or haven't posted anything for a month ... save your money and move on.

What do I suggest? Create your own "targeted" media list for optimum results.

. . .

You'll use your exclusive list to send out pitches and press releases to announce your launch, updates and final days of the campaign.

Read all about it in the next chapter.

8

DIY: DO IT YOURSELF MEDIA LIST

How do you find the right media to contact? BLOGGERS ARE YOUR FRIENDS.

. . .

Remember, no need to re-invent the wheel. Follow tried and true methods that work. Here's some worth doing:

Locate Bloggers/Journalists who want to hear about your project by:

1. Find successful Kickstarter projects that are similar to yours.

2. Look for their main image jpg.

3. Copy and paste that image to your desktop.

4. Now drag that image into images.google.com.

5. What you'll find is articles/links about this project covered by the media, bloggers.

. . .

6. Now copy those links and contact THE SAME BLOGGERS, JOURNALISTS about your project.

7. Be sure to have a short and sweet pitch ready.

8. The best part about this: You already know they're interested in your project because they covered something like it before.

List your top 10 bloggers who are most likely to promote your project:

- 1. _____
- 2. _____
- 3. _____
- 4. _____
- 5. _____
- 6. _____
- 7. _____
- 8. _____
- 9. _____
- 10. _____

Although I am only asking for 10, this should

just be a start for you. Consider compiling a list of 75-200 bloggers. Be sure to target both large and small bloggers. (*Large bloggers have a wider audience, however, they may be less responsive. Smaller bloggers have micro audiences, but they may be more responsive to you*).

When approaching them, always phrase the pitch as to why their audience would be interested; **what is in it for them.** *Make it all about them.*

• Ninja Outreach (https://ninjaoutreach.com/) may be a tool to consider. For $99 a month you can find bloggers by niche, their stats, followers and contact information.

• Another resource is Buzzstream.com. It's a blogger outreach tool. They help you build word-of-mouth and develop relationships with influencers.

• There is also a fantastic article I came across, "30 People to Promote Your Kickstarter or Indiegogo to on Twitter." (http://www.crowdcrux.com/30-

people-to-promote-your-kickstarter-or-indiegogo-
campaign-to-on-twitter/)

It's an older article, but may still be useful to
you. Please don't simply tweet them about your
project. Follow them, read their tweets, see what
interests them prior to asking a favor.

• Don't forget LinkedIn.com. Search for "Reporter" as a title and narrow search within 30 mile
radius of your zip code. Add other key words to
narrow the search.

NOTE: If you are already on LinkedIn, consider creating a group for your campaign and in-
vite people, and/or join other active groups who
would be interested in your project, or are crowd-
funders themselves.

• Alltop (http://alltop.com/about/) You can think of
Alltop as the "online magazine rack" of the web.
Use it as a ramped up RSS feed. It will show top
outlets and blogs, according to subject. Pick sub-
jects relevant to your project and use to build your
media list.

. . .

• HARO (http://www.helpareporter.com/); short for Help a Reporter Out. Sign up for free. When a reporter is looking for an expert on a subject, they post here. If you don't fit into what they are looking for, create a list of reporters who post on your subject, then send them a pitch outside of HARO. Owned by Vocus; an EXPENSIVE service for marketing purposes. Skip Vocus, use the free HARO service.

• Kicktraq.com - enter your Kickstarter project link here for further exposure. Also tracks your analytics. Another free service.

9

ONE LINE PRESS RELEASE

Have you heard of the "one line" press release? It's a simple one liner, designed to peak interest. Always includes a link to a full release, or simply your crowdfunding project page.

. . .

A unique resource is MUCK RACK (https://muck-rack.com/pitching-outreach). With Muck Rack Pro, it is now simple to locate, monitor and pitch to journalists and bloggers who are most interested in your story. Search for them by topic, publication, beat and even what they link to. They used to be $99 a month, but now they are hiding their pricing, which to me says they are expensive. But, you may only need a short period of time to locate the journalists who are right for you. *Ask them for a free trial.*

FREE places to post your press releases:
    1. PRLog - (https://www.prlog.org/)
    2. Free-Press-Release.com
    3. NewsWireToday.com
    4. PR.com
    5. OnlinePRNews.com (Free, $22 and up)

QUIZ: Is Your Press Release Sharable? Circle the correct responses.

1. How long should a press release be?

    a. One page
    b. Two pages
    c. Three pages

2. Using industry jargon within your press releases reinforces your expertise.
    a. True
    b. False

3. What is the most important factor your press releases should include?
    a. Perfect punctuation and grammar
    b. Explicit details on the company behind the campaign
    c. Professional graphics, images and/or videos
    d. Information that is relevant to specific audiences and timely

4. When is the best time to send a press release to a daily newspaper or online outlet?
    a. At night
    b. First thing in the morning
    c. In the afternoon

d. Anytime

5. *You should send the same press release to every outlet for continuity.*
    a. True
    b. False

How do you think you did?

ANSWERS:

1. A - Your press release should be 300-500 words or one page at the most. Reporters/bloggers spend on average one minute reading these. get to the point with as few words as possible.

2. False - You may lose your audience who may find it pretentious or may not understand it.

3. D - Relevant and timely information will create urgency and interest in your campaign.

4. B - when reporters are looking for the stories they want to focus on for the day.

5. False - you should tweak your press releases and personalize them in some way when sending them directly to the media or bloggers.

.   .   .

SCORING:

4-5 Correct - You're on top of your game

3 Correct - You need to brush up

1-2 Correct - Whoops! You really need this book!

10

SAMPLE PITCH

So what does a SAMPLE PITCH look like? It should have the following elements:

· · ·

1. Be personalized to the recipient, no: *To Whom It May Concern*, or *Dear Editorial Department*

2. Have a Short, Intriguing Subject Line

3. Short Introduction of Who You Are

4. Why You Contacted This Person, specifically

5. Complement Them on Past Articles or Works, if possible

6. Tell Them About Your Project and Why They Should Be Interested

7. Close With a **STRONG** Call to Action

8. Attach Image Cover art if you are pitching a book/video game, photo of prototype if you have

invented something, etc. Be sure the image isn't overly large and bulky as you don't want someone deleting your email because it takes too long to download or they believe it's spam.

11

SAMPLE EMAIL PITCH

Dear Michael J. Fox:

My name is Jane Doe and I'm the co-founder of

"Back to the Suture," a Kickstarter Project that aims to raise funds for a revolutionary new product that allows non-medical staff to suture wounds in the field.

I have to say that you have been a big part of my young adulthood. I have followed your career/humanitarian efforts from Family Ties to your research to eradicate Parkinson disease. I believe your drive to fund the necessary research has made a vast improvement to the lives of those suffering from it.

In fact, that is why I have contacted you. We read at *http://www.madeup-blogger-website.com* that you are fascinated by new medical breakthroughs of all kinds.

Will you will take a few moments to view the preview link of our project on Kickstarter? We would love your opinion as well as a short mention of our project though your social media channels.

. . .

We urge you to contact us, via email or phone, prior to our launch date of XXX, 2020.

Warmest regards,
    Jane Doe,
    JaneDoe@notarealemail.com
    310-555-1212
    Insert Kickstarter Project Link HERE

That's it. Brief, detailed and to the point.

Now it's your turn. Write your pitch below. Be sure to include all the points mentioned above.

_____

_____

_____

_____

_____

_____

_____

_____

_____

_____

NOTES:

12

32 PLACES TO PROMOTE YOUR CAMPAIGN ONLINE

Although most of the work will have to be done by you and/or your team, there are a few websites that lend a helping hand in getting the word out about your project.

Reviewed and updated in 2019.

. . .

1.   Crowdfunding   Forum   (http://crowdfundingforum.com/forum.php) - A great place to hang out, look for free programs, resources, get advice, post your project.

2. Crowdfunding Hub (http://ow.ly/S74ys) - Become a member of this google+ group, then post your project. Campaigns are divided up according to where you launched. (May go away once Google dissolves Google+). Try to contribute to the discussion before posting.

3. Google Groups (https://groups.google.com/forum/#!search/kickstarter) - Search for groups using keywords "Kickstarter," "Indiegogo," "Crowdfunding." I did not include Yahoo groups with this listing as a recent search turned up a handful of groups with less than 20 members. Not worth your time.

4. Guest Blogging: Find a blogger or two.(*Use DIY: Do It Yourself Media List Chapter for instructions.*)

Ask if you can be a guest blogger on their site. Write relevant articles with useful information ON A WEEKLY BASIS FOR AT LEAST 10 WEEKS.

With every posting, be sure to list your contact information, including a website/landing page for your upcoming campaign, and of course, make the newsletter subscription prominent on your website/landing page.

5. Simply writing one post will not get you a following. 10 or more will. One campaigner gathered over 100,000 followers/emails (http://ow.ly/S74IK) over the course of nine months from this tip alone. Want another place to find bloggers who are looking for guest articles?

Try MyBlogGuest.com. This is a free service where you can post articles and have other bloggers ask to publish your article on their website. You can also search for useful articles and get permission to publish their articles on your blog. (*In order to use this service, you must have a blog of your own*).

. . .

You may also want to do a search for Kickstarter within Twitter, Pinterest and Facebook.

6. Crowdfunding Projects: http://crowdfunding. stream/submit: Vote for top projects, submit your own for free and more.

7. Kicktraq.com - Enter the URL of your campaign (or a similar campaign currently running) on their home page. Now view the pledge history of the campaign or see how the campaign is trending and if it's likely to fund. They also have free browser add-ons for Chrome and Firefox. Additionally, consider submitting stories about your project and it might show up on their home page to garner further exposure.

8. Linkedin.com- Search for their crowdfunding groups and join the discussion, post comments, ask for advice.

9. Fiverr.com - This site has marketers who will publicize your project, FUND your project and

more. Simply search using keywords: Kickstarter, Indiegogo or Crowdfunding. Find support starting at $5!

10. Crowdsunite.com - helps you choose the best crowdfunding site for your project and also lets you advertise your project on their site for free

11. Crowd101 - https://www.crowd101.com/crowd-101-blog/ - list of places to submit your campaign to for exposure.

12. Reddit.com - is a social bookmark website. Search for sub-groups with the words Kickstarter, Indiegogo, Crowdfunding, etc.

13. The Backer Club - https://backerclub.co/homepage.php A place to pitch and promote your project to serial backers for Kickstarter and In-diegogo. Can submit your project in pre-launch or launched phase.

. . .

14. Pinterest.com - Simply join boards that have themes similar to your projects. Example: If you are crowdfunding for a video game, find boards with "video games" as the keyword and follow. They may do the same in return. Post images of your prototypes, box covers, people interacting with your game, etc.

15. Buzzfeed.com - Promoting here is as easy as registering on the site and creating a post on your dashboard. Buzzfeed has promoted several crowd-funding campaigns.

16. Hyperstarter - https://www.hyperstarter.com/ - FREE! Just plug in the link to your Kickstarter campaign and this s-ware will review your page for quality and identify issues.

17. Kickstarterforum.org - Post campaign news.

18. Pitch to your local newspaper, or local shopper magazine/paper. Be sure to do this several months

prior to your launch to give them adequate time to include your product.

19. BackersHub.com - Offers members discounts on crowdfunded products.

20. Kickbooster.me - Allows campaign creators to run a referral program during their crowdfunding campaign and provides incentive for Boosters (backers or affiliates) to share and promote your campaign.

21. BetaList.com - The place for early adopters to discover upcoming internet startups, and for startup founders to share their startup with the world and get early user feedback. Increases your mailing list. Can only be used when your campaign is in pre-launch phase and when you have a website to send the traffic to.

22. Thunderclap.it - The first-ever crowd-speaking platform that helps people be heard by saying something together.

. . .

23. Gadget Flow - https://thegadgetflow.com/submit/ Gadget Flow is the original product discovery platform for staying up to date with the latest tech, gear, and most incredible crowdfunding campaigns. Boost your exposure and find targeted audiences.

24. Green Inbox - https://www.greeninbox.com/ Helps boost your funding through targeted facebook ads and personally emailing your facebook friends and gmail friends (without appearing in the promotions tab).

25. Crowdfunding Exposure - https://crowdfundingexposure.com/free-crowdfunding-promotion-promote-my-crowdfunding-campaign-for-free/ Submit your project using the FREE option to help get the word out. You'll need to complete a form on your project.

26. Crowdfundbuzz.com - https://www.crowdfundbuzz.com/ They generate PR and social

media content for crowdfunding campaigns. To be honest, their site sucks big time. So if you decide to give them a try, don't spend too much. Test them out first. They do require you to complete a form online. *Ask for a free trial at that time.*

27. Product Hunt - https://www.producthunt.com/promoted-products Get your product in front of the tech community, reaching millions of founders, investors, reporters, and makers every month. You may even want to sign up to be a "maker."

28. Cool Backer - https://coolbacker.com/submit-your-project-for-a-sponsored-post/ They list the "coolest" crowdfunding projects around. They support projects utilizing gadgets, tech, clothing, transportation and more.

29. Oddity Central - http://www.odditycentral.com/tip-us-off Have an odd or unique campaign? Submit it here.

. . .

30. The Startup Pitch - https://thestartuppitch. com/post-a-pitch/ They created a site where people could go and post startup-related stories without having to have a blog.

31. HyperStarter - https://www.hyperstarter.com/ find-crowdfunding-influencers This site requires an email before they send you a list of the top 150+ influencers to promote your crowdfunding campaign too. (*I have not read the current report. If you have, drop me a note and let me know if you think it's worthwhile or not*).

32. Krowdster - https://www.krowdster.co/ Promote your crowdfunding campaign through their list of backers, facebook audience, media list and more.

Which ones seem like a fit for your campaign? Why?

_____

_____

_____

_____

_____

. . .

List "must-have" features before researching and selecting your partners. (*Example: must be free, been in business X number of years, qualified references, services, timely response, specific audience, etc.*)

_____

_____

_____

_____

_____

_____

13

SPECIAL TIPS TO GRAB FUNDERS' ATTENTION

• Consider creating an infographic to explain your project, or your perks. People love pictures more than they like to read. Make it fun and interesting to get to know you and your project. **So what is an**

infographic? Infographics are graphics that relay information in a flowchart. Here is a basic example (http://www.kickstarter.com/projects/ajleon/the-life-and-times-of-a-remarkable-misfit) of one used by a writer on Kickstarter, which helped him raise $38,000.

You can create one for FREE at PiktoChart.com. *(PiktoChart offers simple templates for the free service. The more advanced features require paid membership).* Or you can hire someone to do it for you. Upwork.com is a great place to post cheap jobs and get multiple bids. Canva.com also has infographic templates which make it easy to create one on the fly. *The service is also free.*

• On your Kickstarter Page, there are links under the main video for visitors to LIKE, TWEET and EMBED. Draw attention to those links/buttons in your video. In the video, point down to where they are located and ask for the SHARE, or LIKE.

• Create a graphic with arrows that point up to the video with the words "Watch My Video," or

"Check out my Video." Some people completely miss the video and don't know it's there. To see an example, go to: http://www.kickstarter.com/projects/597507018/pebble-e-paper-watch-for-iphone-and-android?ref=live. It's the wrapped Kickstarter page for the infamous Pebble Watch which raised a staggering $10,266,845.00.

• Create a sense of urgency by offering a reward that is limited to an X number of backers. Make it something that will cost more once it's available to the public.

• Offer Limited Editions, or personalized items, for an X number of backers.

• About one week before your project closes, add a $1 reward, offering people exclusive updates and news. This can create a healthy and substantially targeted email list.

How will you grab possible backers attention?

. . .

Assignment:

- Email your current friends, associates and family
- Tell them about your crowdfunding campaign idea
- Ask them what they would like to see as an incentive for backing your project
- Take notes and create a top 10 list
- Ask them to vote for their favorites and to tell you "why" they are their favorites

What were their favorites? Which ones were perceived as more valuable?

_____

_____

_____

_____

_____

_____

_____

14

HOW TO GET FEATURED ON KICKSTARTER'S AND INDIEGOGO'S WEBSITE AND NEWSLETTER

I receive a weekly newsletter from Kickstarter and Indiegogo which features projects they love. I have personally selected several projects to fund after seeing the pitch in the newsletter. I would never have known about these projects without the newsletter.

So how does your project get selected for the coveted spot in their newsletters? Certainly not by emailing them, asking to be featured. They know projects selected are almost guaranteed funding success.

So here's how it's done.

Look for the link CURATED PAGES (https://www.kickstarter.com/discover/curated-pages?ref=sidebar) on Kickstarter.com. *What are curated projects?* They are creative communities that support projects on Kickstarter.

Look for an organization on that page that fits within your project's subject matter, goals, etc.

Example: Geek Dads; https://www.kickstarter.com/

pages/geekdad They love gadgets, board games, video games, and things they can share with our kids. Have a product that would fit their criteria? Then reach out to them on their website with a well-thought out pitch requesting they add your campaign to their supported projects.

HOW TO REACH OUT TO CURATED COMMUNITIES:

1. Make a list of Curator Communities that fit your project.

2. Locate their website.

3. Contact them, via email or phone, asking if your project can be considered as part of their curated page on Kickstarter.

4. Follow the rules for submission.

. . .

5. Repeat with each appropriate community.

You will find someone who is willing to take you on. Once safely under their umbrella, ask them how your project can be considered for inclusion in the Kickstarter newsletter.

They may, in fact, suggest your project to Kickstarter on your behalf. Now wouldn't that be awesome?!

Another little know fact: *If you've gathered your tribe, ask them to fund your project within the first few days.* If you reach half your funding goal, your campaign will be featured on the home page of Kickstarter, under "Popular" campaigns. This will give you a ton of extra exposure.

What about Indiegogo? They do not have curated pages and depend more on "popularity" or "gogo-factor" when selecting their featured projects.

. . .

Here is what one of the representatives shared with me:

Thanks for your question. Search rankings, placement on the site, featured spots in our newsletter or blog and inclusion in our press outreach are all determined by gogofactor. Indiegogo is a merit-based platform, which means that campaigns earn featured spots by staying active. We do not curate campaigns, nor do we offer paid placement. Your visibility on the site is controlled entirely by you and your community.

Your gogofactor is a rolling average, so it is important to continually keep your campaign active. Your campaign is ranked relative to all of the other campaigns on the site. By staying active, your gogofactor will continue to go up. The more you share and update, and the more community shares, comments and funds, the higher your campaign rises on the browse pages and the greater the chance you will have of getting featured.

For more information about the gogofactor and

links to tips on how to run a successful campaign, go here: https://support.indiegogo.com/hc/en-us/articles/527476-The-Gogofactor .

There you have it. Multiple ways to attract the big bucks to your project.

ASSIGNMENT:

- Go to: https://www.kickstarter.com/discover/curated-pages?ref=sidebar
- Search for curated pages under the categories which best fit your project
- Make a list of possible curators

List your possible curators below and check them off as you reach out to them:

— _____

— _____

— _____

— _____

— _____

— _____

— _____

— _____

— _____

— _____

— _____

— _____

— _____

— _____

— _____

— _____

— _____

— _____

— _____

— _____

— _____

— _____

— _____

— _____

15

16 SUREFIRE TIPS FOR RELAUNCHING A FAILED CAMPAIGN - IF AT FIRST YOU DON'T SUCCEED...

So you've discovered this book AFTER your campaign fizzled. No worries. In fact, you may be in better shape than someone who hasn't gone through what you have. How so? Hopefully, you've unintentionally learned a few things. Take that knowledge and try again!

Here are a few tips to get you going:

1. Have a friend/colleague compare your campaign to others currently running in your category. Ask him/her what they have that yours doesn't. (Be open to constructive criticism).

2. Take a closer look at your video. Is it all about you or the product? If it's all about you, dump it and try spending more time on the product, giving visual details. Demonstrate how the product benefits the user/backer; keeping it short and simple. Try to keep the video within one to four minutes. Under one minute, it's a commercial, over four minutes; a documentary.

3. Rethink your funding goal. Too high? Too low?

. . .

4. Is your "story" compelling enough? If not, come up with a new story or tweak the one you have. People want to connect with you. Give them a reason to do so.

5. Pie in the sky ideas. I'm not one to crush anyone's dreams, but you have to be realistic. If your goal is to raise $500,000 to end world hunger by handing out smiley pins to kids in Uganda ... it probably won't happen. Set reasonable expectations and goals.

6. You misunderstood your target audience. Before embarking on another crowdfunding campaign, think about the audience you are trying to reach. How much do you really know about them? Do your research.

7. You misdirected your campaign. Yes, you know all about the product you are trying to sell, or the movie you are trying to make, but does your audience? Put yourself in their shoes, then explain it in a way that is understandable to an audience who has never heard of you or your project.

. . .

8. Was your message clear and concise? Or did it get lost amongst all the other campaigns? Make yours stand out by avoiding generic stories, descriptions of your product, etc. Find keywords that fit your campaign specifically. Use in all of your marketing, as well as the actual campaign page.

Example: You have created an app that will help you lose weight. *Instead of, "Lose Weight With My App," try, "Busy Mothers Lose 10 pounds in Just 10 Minutes a Day with XX App."*

9. Did you follow-up with everyone who left comments or contacted you? Did you follow-up the same day? I've visited websites where I was very interested in buying a certain product, but I had questions. So I emailed them and waited, and waited. If I don't hear back from them within 1 day, I write them off. People may have written you off as well if you have poor follow-up skills.

10. Is your project crowd-fundable? Maybe it's not. Maybe there are just too few people interested in cats made with toothpicks. You're better off finding alternative funds for your niche product elsewhere.

11. **Take a look at your campaign page.** Is it too overly complicated? Do you drown people in information with blocks upon blocks of information? Or is it overly simplified with not enough information? It should be visually exciting and stimulating. Highlight the benefits of the product; how it functions using illustrations, banners and text with lots of white space.

12. **Don't throw out the failed campaign.** You did generate interest. Leverage that interest by adding a link on your updates page (story page cannot be changed once campaign closes) to a NEW VIDEO where you ask your supporters to back your new crowdfunding campaign. Be sure to address what will/has changed to get them excited about it. *Don't simply copy and paste old campaign to the new one.* There was a reason why it failed and you must address that.

13. **Did you put in enough time?** Crowdfunding

campaigns take a lot of time and energy. Be sure to put in the additional time on reformulating your campaign, marketing and outreach.

14. Ask other successful crowdfunding campaign creators for feedback. Choose campaigns similar to yours. They may also be able to share techniques which worked for them. You may be able to reach them through their closed campaign pages, or simply googling their product to find their website.

ASSIGNMENT:

- Right now, do a google search on "successful crowdfunding campaigns"
- Look for ones similar to the one you will be launching
- Write down their contact information
- Reach out to them, ask if you can have a few minutes of their time to discuss their crowdfunding campaign (*in exchange for adding them as a partner on your website and inclusion in your newsletter with a link to their "closed"*

campaign or website... or something else of value to them)

- Once you have them on the phone, ask them why they believe their campaign was a success and advice they can share with you

You may also want to check out my companion book, KICKASS KICKSTARTER GODS (https://www.patricewilliamsmarks.com/product/kickass-kickstarter-gods-2/) ; which includes interviews with many mega-successful crowdfunding campaigners who shared their secrets to raising thousands, even millions of dollars for through their campaigns. Learn from people who have done what you are striving to achieve.

Write down your top 5 questions below that you will be asking:

1. _____

_____

2. _____

_____

3. _____

4. _____

5. _____

15. Back other projects. Doing so not only gives you good karma, but also allows you to personally comment on their comments page; asking them for advice or helpful hints. They will be more apt to respond when they see that you are a backer.

16. Create a contest giveaway for your product prior to your launch. This gives you tons of free publicity and new places to promote. It also gives you a quick way to build up your mailing list. There are several companies, (such as *Rafflecopter* or *Gleam)* which can be used to run your contest.

16

TOO MUCH FOR ONE PERSON TO HANDLE?

It is a hell of a lot of work. But making money only comes easily for a select few. However, if you have a spare $100 a month, I have a great suggestion.

Hire a virtual assistant.

. . .

A company called Zirtual.com has screened workers who take on small to large projects at affordable prices. For as little as $97 a month, you can hire someone to do all your internet work for you.

There are other companies as well who do the same thing. Or, you can find someone at Upwork.com .

Simply give them detailed instructions and voilà, you get an extra set of hands. Ask your virtual assistant to find people to follow on your new Twitter account, Facebook account, etc., or have him/her do research for you in creating a targeted media or blogger list. The sky's the limit.

Go forth, grasshopper, and prosper.

THE END

17

WRAP-UP

I sincerely hope this ebook has served you well. Please email me at pwm@patricewilliamsmarks.com with suggestions, or the like. I would especially appreciate hearing about your successfully funded projects using

the techniques featured in this ebook. I would love to feature them in an updated version.

Also: Drop me a line when you are ready to launch your project. I'll select several projects throughout the year to promote on my social media channels for free. *(Please note that I cannot promote every project. ALSO, YOU MUST BE A SUBSCRIBER TO MY NEWSLETTER LIST TO QUALIFY).*

SUBSCRIBE (http://www.patricewilliamsmarks.com/home-referral)

Remember: **REVIEWS are always welcome on all bookstores.** (goo.gl/yvFyEq)

LIST OF CROWDFUNDING WEBSITES

This list has been verified and updated for 2019. New ones have been added while others have been removed. *Do your homework to select the best fit for your project.*

Boostup - https://www.boostup.com/ Saving for your new car and home just got easier

Causes - https://www.causes.com/ Support the people and causes that inspire you. Campaign to make a difference.

CrowdCube - http://www.crowdcube.com/ Funding platform for UK businesses and investors

Crowdfunder   -   https://www.crowdfunder.-com/Caters to entrepreneurs and small-business owners who need capital

Crowdrise - http://www.Crowdrise.com Raise money for causes that inspire you

Crowdsunite - http://crowdsunite.com/ Helps you choose the best crowdfunding site for your project and also lets you advertise your project on their site for free

DonorsChoose - http://www.DonorsChoose.org Designed to help teachers raise money for under-funded public schools

Fairstreet - https://www.fairstreet.com/ All types of projects

Fundable - https://www.fundable.com/ Raising funding capital from investors for small business

Funder Hut - http://www.funderhut.com/ A community-oriented crowdfunding platform that helps support small businesses, nonprofits, local communities, and individuals looking to fundraise

Fundly - https://fundly.com/ Raise money for anything

Fundrazr - http://www.Fundrazr.com Flexible contribution platform that makes it possible to start campaigns for nearly any cause

GiveForward / GoFundme - https://www.giveforward.com/ and http://www.gofundme.com/ Specializes in personal stories, medical or social issues

GoGetFunding - http://www.GoGetFunding.com Specializes in personal causes and events

Indiegogo - http://www.indiegogo.com/ All types of projects

Jewcer - http://jewcer.com/ Supporting projects that benefit the Jewish Community

Kickstarter - http://www.kickstarter.com/ All types of projects

Medstarter - http://www.medstartr.com/ Patients, doctors, and companies funding healthcare innovation

MicroVentures - http://www.MicroVentures.com Combines venture capital with crowdfunding options for startups

Mighty Cause - https://www.mightycause.com/ Online fundraising software for empowering non-profits, people, and the causes they believe in.

OurCrowd - http://www.OurCrowd.com Equity crowdfunding for startups

Patreon - https://www.patreon.com/ Provides funding services to help creators achieve their goals of supporting themselves with their work

PledgeMusic - http://www.PledgeMusic.com Empowers artists to raise money

Plumfund - http://www.Plumfund.com Crowdfunding sight that best suits people that are looking to raise money for a special occasion

Slated - https://welcome.slated.com/ Where great movies are funded and distributed

Spacehive - http://www.Spacehive.com is the UK's

dedicated crowdfunding platform for places (*based in UK*)

StartSomeGood   -   http://startsomegood.com/ Crowdfunding for socially-responsible projects

Thunderclap - https://www.thunderclap.it/en A tool that lets a message be heard when you and your friends say it together

Ulule - http://www.ulule.com/ Specializing in innovative, creative projects

YouCaring   -   Now   https://GoFundMe.com fundraising for good

WeFunder - https://wefunder.com/ Specializing in startup funding.

COMPANION BOOK

From the author of HACKING KICKSTARTER &
INDIEGOGO: SECRETS TO RUNNING A SUC-
CESSFUL CROWDFUNDING CAMPAIGN ON A
BUDGET comes a companion book, KICKASS

KICKSTARTER GODS: Experts Reveal Their Pathways to Millions Through Crowdfunding.

Kickass Kickstarter Gods interviewed creators of mega-successful crowdfunding campaigns that made six and seven figures, and asked them:

1. Why was your campaign successful?

2. How far in advance did you plan out your campaign?

3. What was your strategy?

4. How did you decide which platform to use (Kickstarter, Indiegogo, GoFundMe, etc.)?

5. Any unexpected hurdles or hardships?
   ... and more

THIS IS PURE GOLD. Why reinvent the wheel? Learn from successful crowdfunding campaigners who made their dreams a reality and raised millions to make it happen.

GRAB YOUR COPY NOW!

https://www.patricewilliamsmarks.com/product/kickass-kickstarter-gods-2/

ABOUT THE AUTHOR

JOIN MAILING LIST http://www.patricewilliams-marks.com/home-referral

Patrice Williams Marks penned her first book in third grade: The Day Snoopy Got Married. While it didn't make the New York Times Bestseller List, it was an instant classic with the Nunaka Valley

Elementary School staff. From that moment forward, Patrice knew she was a writer.

With a zest for travel and an insatiable appetite for all things vintage and period, Patrice uses her investigative journalism background to create useful non-fiction how-to books which have become Amazon bestsellers, alongside historical fiction novels. She is also a Sensitivity Reader and teaches others the craft through an online course.

Follow Me:
www.PatriceWilliamsMarks.com
www.SensitivityReviews.com
pwm@patrice@williamsmarks.com

NOTES:

NOTES:

NOTES:

NOTES:

NOTES:

NOTES:

NOTES:

NOTES:

Made in the USA
San Bernardino, CA
12 March 2019